Patterns

Let's Do Math!

Sara Pistoia and
Piper Whelan

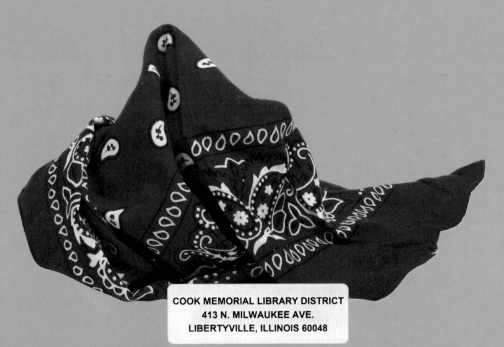

www.av2books.com

AV² provides enriched content that supplements and complements this book. Weigl's AV² books strive to create inspired learning and engage young minds in a total learning experience.

Your AV² Media Enhanced books come alive with...

Audio
Listen to sections of the book read aloud.

Video
Watch informative video clips.

Embedded Weblinks
Gain additional information for research.

Try This!
Complete activities and hands-on experiments.

Key Words
Study vocabulary, and complete a matching word activity.

Quizzes
Test your knowledge.

Slide Show
View images and captions, and prepare a presentation.

...and much, much more!

Go to **www.av2books.com**, and enter this book's unique code.

BOOK CODE

R635549

AV² by Weigl brings you media enhanced books that support active learning.

Published by AV² by Weigl
350 5th Avenue, 59th Floor New York, NY 10118
Website: www.av2books.com

Library of Congress Cataloging-in-Publication Data

Names: Pistoia, Sara- author. I Whelan, Piper- author.
Title: Patterns / Sara Pistoia and Piper Whelan.
Description: New York, NY : AV2 by Weigl, [2017] I Series: Let's do math! I
  Includes index.
Identifiers: LCCN 2016002883 (print) I LCCN 2016007852 (ebook) I ISBN
  9781489651167 (hard cover : alk. paper) I ISBN 9781489651174 (soft cover :
  alk. paper) I ISBN 9781489651181 (Multi-User eBook)
Subjects: LCSH: Pattern perception--Juvenile literature. I Geometry--Juvenile
  literature. I Mathematics--Juvenile literature.
Classification: LCC BF294 .P57 2017 (print) I LCC BF294 (ebook) I DDC
  516.15--dc23
LC record available at http://lccn.loc.gov/2016002883

Printed in the United States of America in Brainerd, Minnesota
1 2 3 4 5 6 7 8 9 0 20 19 18 17 16

072016
210716

Project Coordinator: Piper Whelan
Art Director: Terry Paulhus

The publisher acknowledges iStock and Getty Images as the primary image suppliers for this title.

2

Let's Do Math!

Patterns

In this book, you will learn about

- **where patterns are found**

- **how patterns can be made**

- **what comes next in a pattern**

- **how patterns help us in math**

and much more!

We use patterns to recognize all kinds of things in our world.

Colors or shapes used over and over form a pattern.

You can see patterns on wrapping paper. You can see patterns on leaves and flowers.

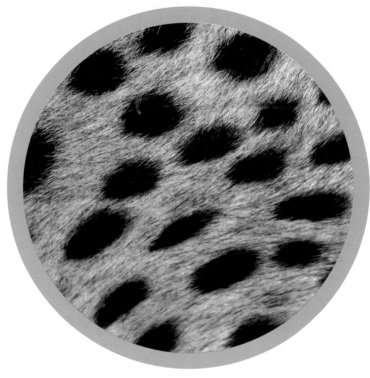

These patterns are on animal fur. Can you guess which animals they are?

The world would be different without patterns.

Without stripes, this zebra would look like a horse!

Tigers and leopards are both wild cats. Is this a tiger or a leopard?

You can tell by the stripes on its fur. Tigers have stripes. Leopards have spots.

Patterns can be made with shapes, sizes, colors, and positions.

Look at the animal on the next page. You know it is a panda because it looks like a panda. But what makes a panda look different from a grizzly bear?

A panda's black and white coloring forms a pattern. That pattern makes the panda look different from every other animal.

Pandas have white faces
with black patches around
their eyes. Where else do
you see black patches?

Sometimes the parts of a pattern repeat themselves.

When patterns repeat, it helps us think about what might come next.

These jelly beans form a pattern. The pattern uses colors and numbers. How can you tell what color comes next?

To figure out which color jelly bean comes next, think about the order of the colors you see.

Next, count how many of each color are there. Red, red, yellow, green. Red, red, yellow, green.

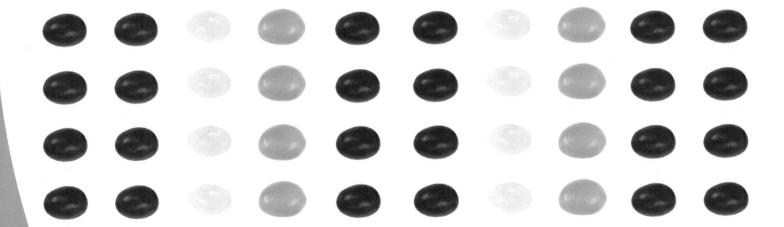

Some patterns are simple, like the stripes on this snake.

Do you see the pattern?
Red, black, yellow, black.
Red, black, yellow, black.

Some patterns are not so simple. This wrapping paper has a pattern, but it keeps changing. Can you tell what might come next?

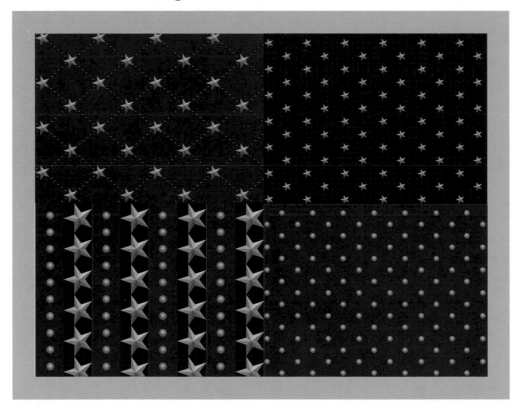

It is hard to know what would come next in this pattern!

Knowing about patterns can help us in math.

When you count, you use a pattern:

0, 1, 2, 3, 4, 5, 6, 7, 8, 9...

What comes next?

Did you say "10"?
You are right!

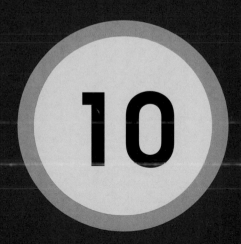

What happens when we reach 10?
The pattern starts all over again!

But this time we put a "1" in front
of each number: 10, 11...

Do you see the pattern?

**10, 11, 12, 13, 14,
15, 16, 17, 18, 19...**

Now try counting the peanuts on the next page.

What happens when we reach 19? We start the pattern all over again at 20.

Can you think of the last four numbers in the pattern?

What comes after 6? What comes after 16? Now think about what comes after 26.

1
2
3
4
5
6
7
8
9
10

11
12
13
14
15
16
17
18
19
20

21
22
23
24
25
26
?
?
?
?

The last four numbers are 27, 28, 29, and 30. Did the pattern change after 29? Yes!

We used the number 3 and started the pattern all over again!

The days of the week form a pattern, too.

Which day always comes after Sunday?

Which day always comes after Wednesday?

Knowing the days of the week can help you solve this math problem:

Say you leave home on Saturday to go to your grandma's house. It will take four days to get there. On what day will you arrive?

Saturday, Sunday, Monday, Tuesday — you will be there Tuesday.

Look at the hundreds chart on this page.

Do you see patterns that can help you with math?

1	2	3	4	5	6	7	8	9	10
11	12	13	14	15	16	17	18	19	20
21	22	23	24	25	26	27	28	29	30
31	32	33	34	35	36	37	38	39	40
41	42	43	44	45	46	47	48	49	50
51	52	53	54	55	56	57	58	59	60
61	62	63	64	65	66	67	68	69	70
71	72	73	74	75	76	77	78	79	80
81	82	83	84	85	86	87	88	89	90
91	92	93	94	95	96	97	98	99	100

Count the numbers with jelly beans. You are counting by fives. What about the last row? Do you know where to place the jelly beans to finish the pattern?

The yellow jelly bean numbers on this chart make a pattern that counts by fives. Study the pattern.

The numbers in the last row must be 95 and 100.

This musician thinks about patterns when she plays or writes music. Scientists think about finding patterns when they study plants. Artists think about patterns when they create a work of art.

Patterns of letters helped you to learn to read. Discovering and using patterns is important in math, too!

If you start thinking about patterns, you can see them everywhere!

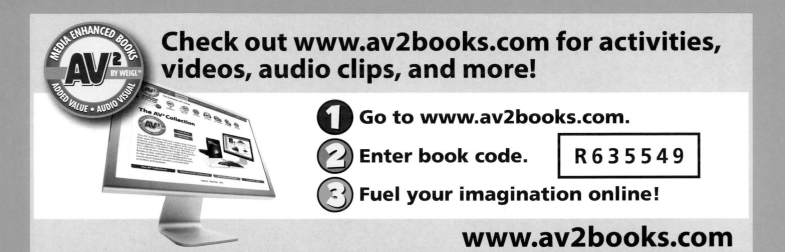

W9-AAZ-318